# Don't
# the Baby



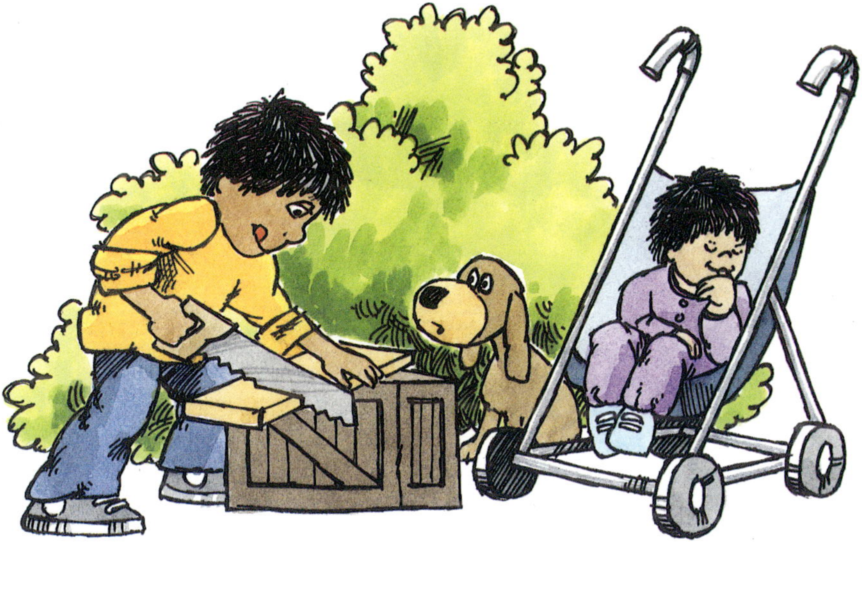

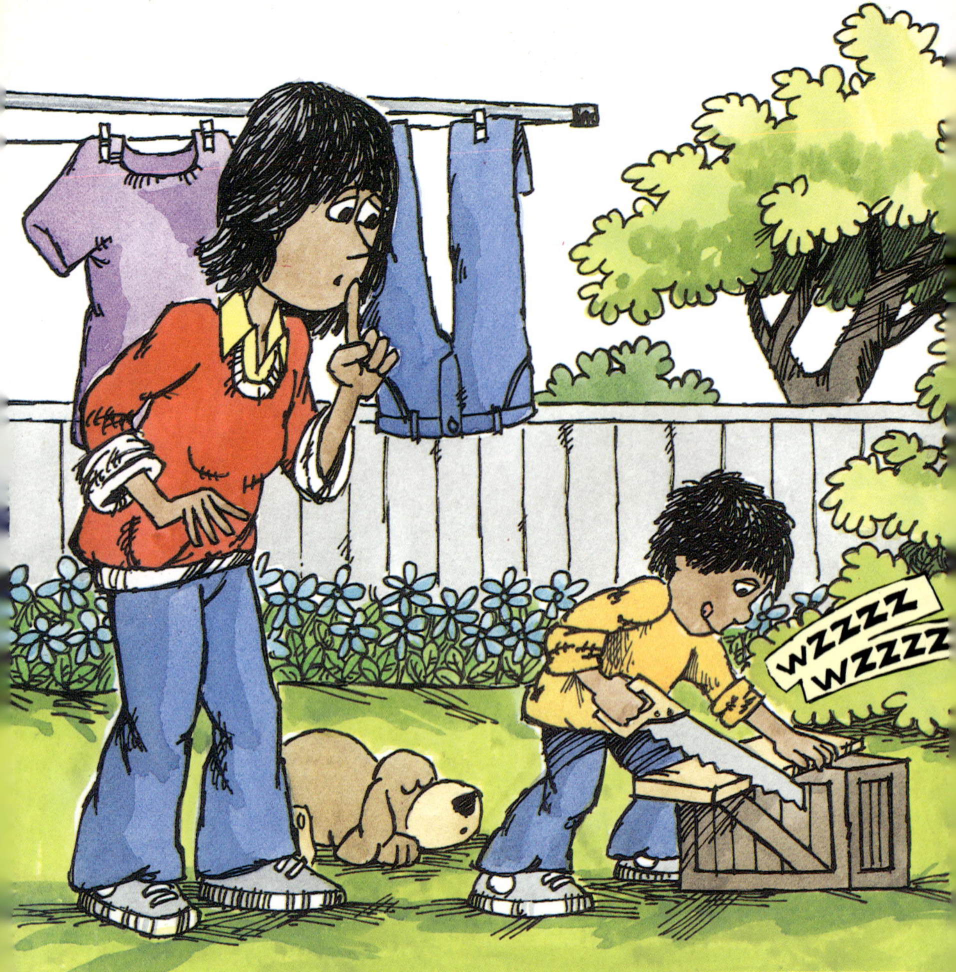


Shh!

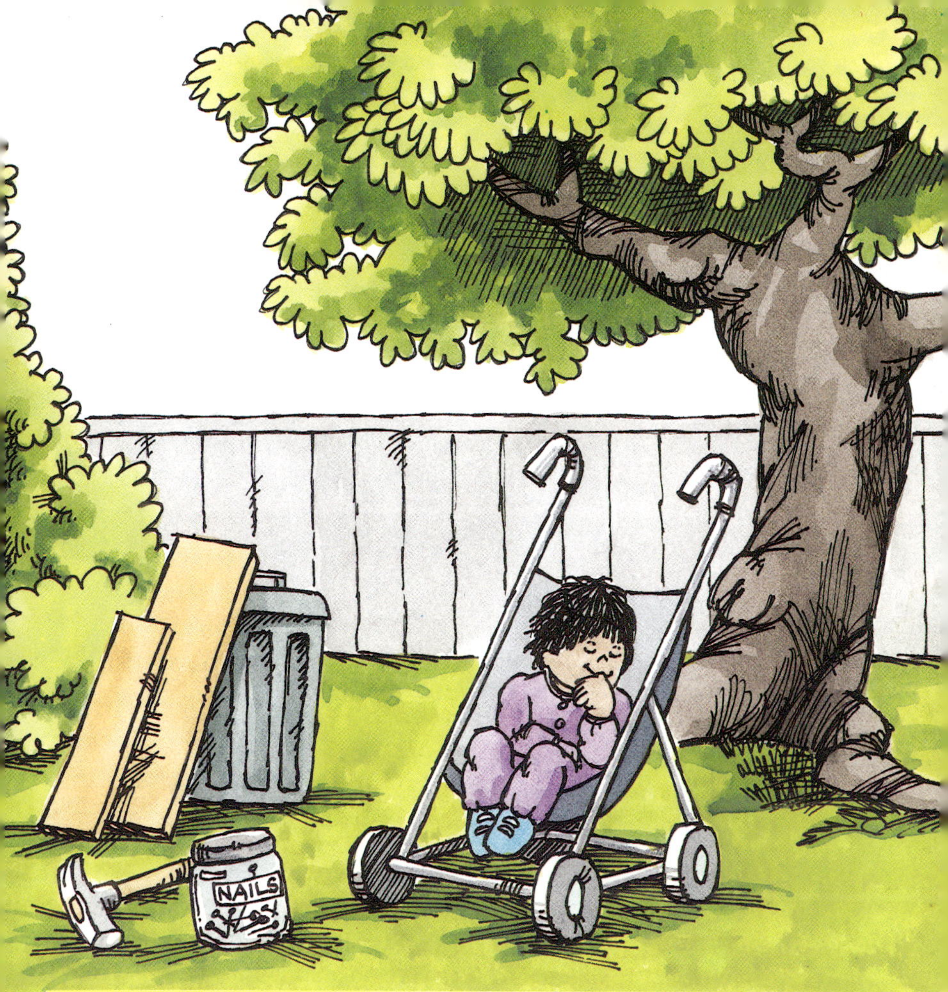


Don't wake the baby.

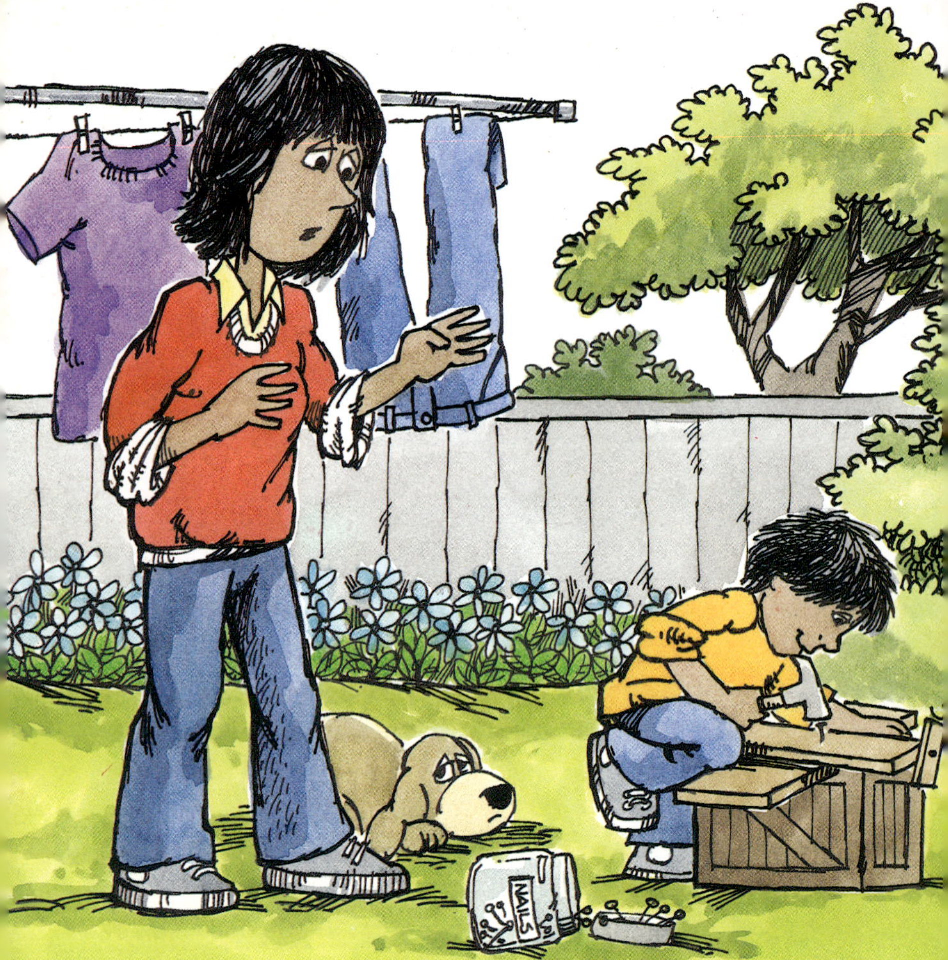


Shhh!

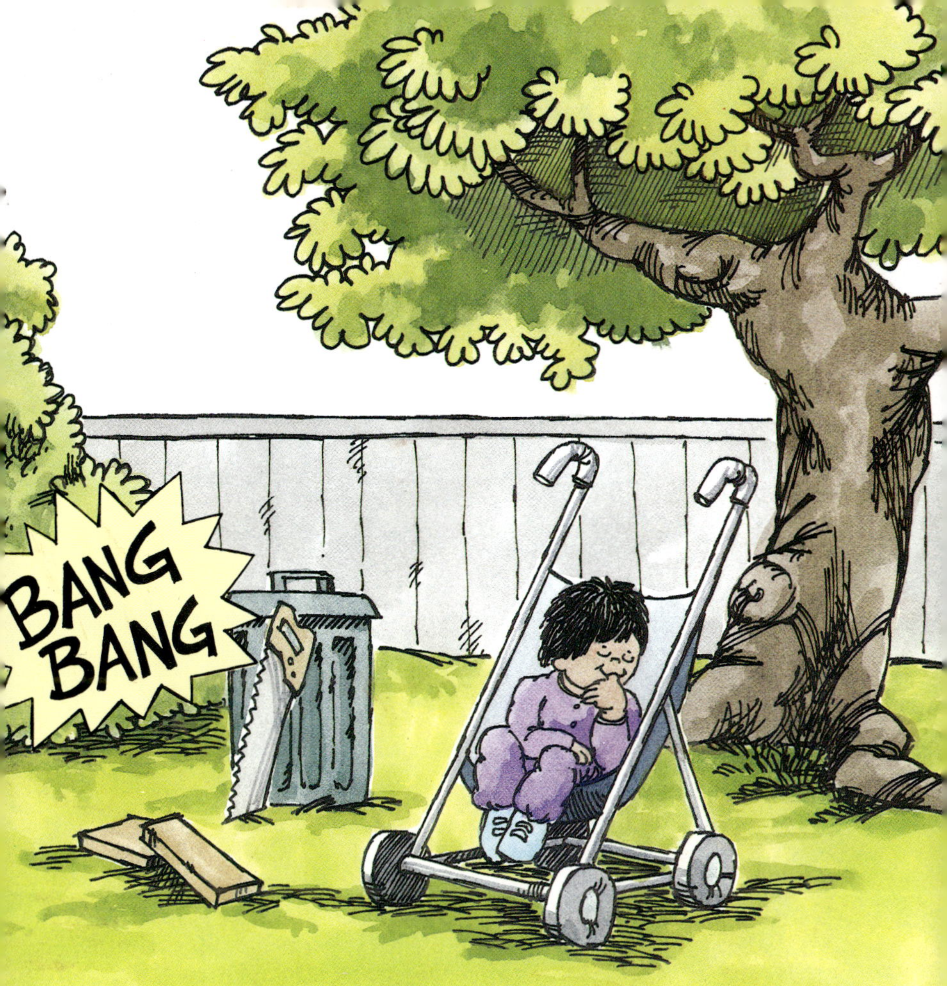


Don't wake the baby.

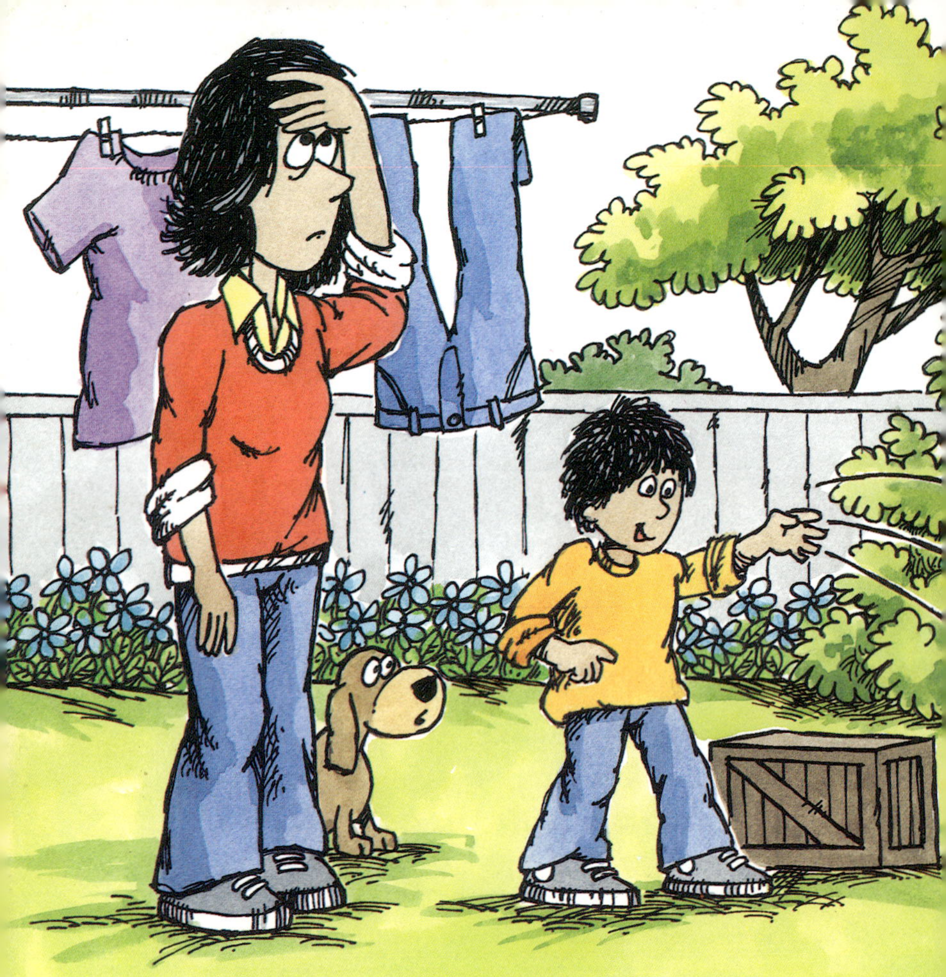

Shhhh!

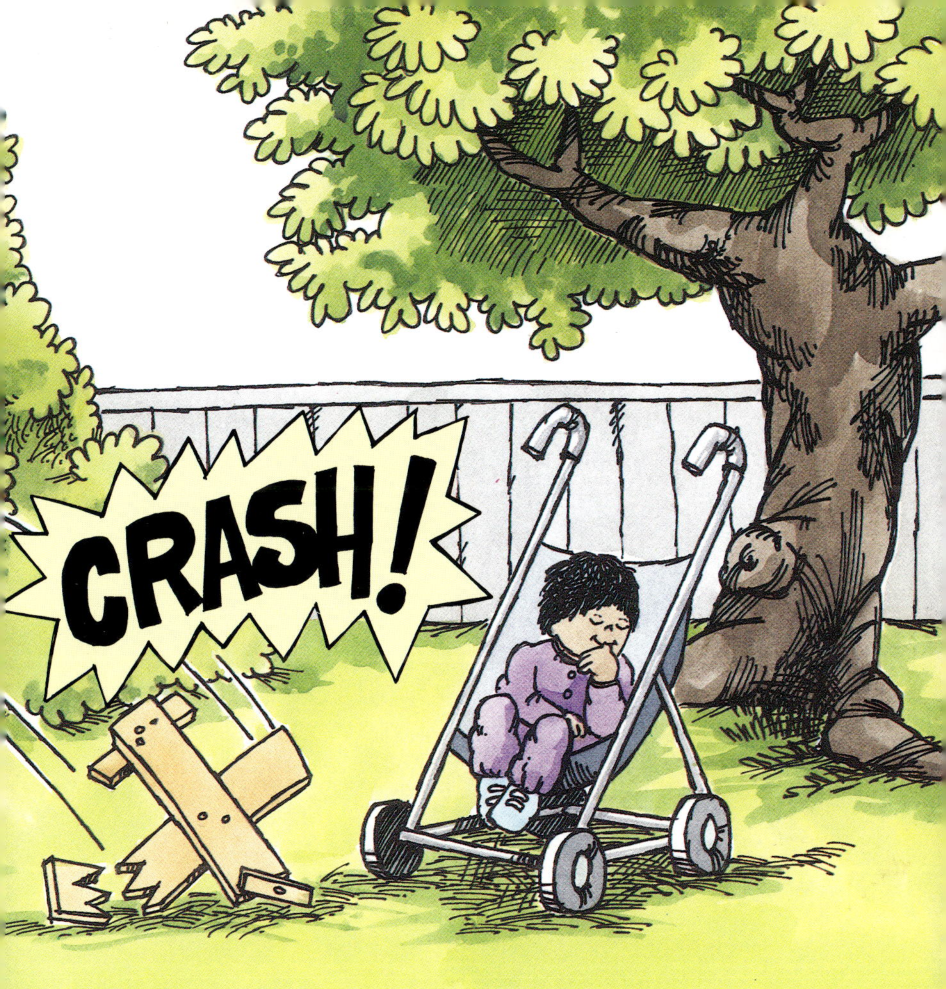


Don't wake the baby.

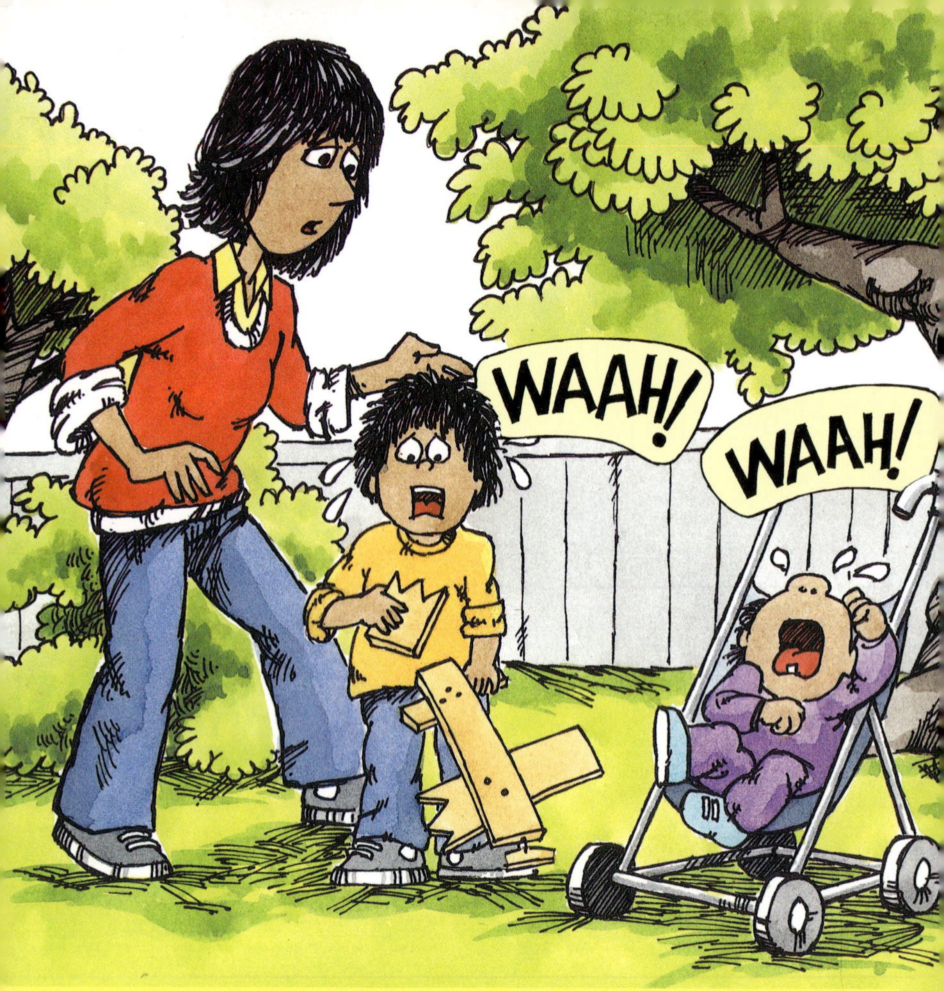


Shhhhh! Too late!